Marketing Magic

100 Magical Ideas to Grow Your Business

Manny Sarmiento

All rights reserved. Published by New Media, New Marketing. No part of this book may be reproduced or transmitted in any form or by any means, electronic or mechanical, including photocopying, recording, or by any information storage and retrieval system, without permission from the publisher. For information address The Marketing Annex Inc, 2900 NW 112th Ave, Miami, Florida, 33172

Printed in the United States of America
First Paperback Edition, December 2017

Designed by Manny Sarmiento

Library of Congress Control Number for Paperback Edition
ISBN: 978-0-9997223-1-2

For Nana, Tata and Carmen

This book is dedicated to Nana, Tata and Carmen!

Who else but Nana (mom) could've believed more in me and make my amazing life possible? I miss Nana every day. I've worked hard for many years to become an amazing success to make Nana and Tata proud. Nana left us too soon. I wanted her to experience my success, but I know that she's watching from Heaven. So here it is, Nana.

Nana has always been my number one motivation to continue working hard and to succeed. Thank you, Nana! I Love You and Miss You Deeply!

Thank you, Tata. You are strong, caring and you dedicated your life to your family. You took care of Nana till the end! You are an inspiration to me and many others. I love you.

To Carmen, my love, my backbone, my inspiration! You are strong. You are beautiful! You are incredible! You are an inspiration! This book is dedicated to you because you have always been there for me. I love you dearly.

God Bless all my friends and everyone who's been there for me through the good times and bad times. I love you all!

Table of Contents

Preface...11

Mystify Your Audience with Great Customer Service....12

Under Promise and Over Deliver!...14

Zig when they Zag!...15

Use Every Door Direct Mail EDDM....16

Join a Chamber of Commerce....17

Build Relationships!...18

Understand How Social Media Really Works!...19

Get A Linkedin Profile!...21

Join 10 Groups On Linkedin....22

Participate In 2 Discussions On Linkedin Groups!...23

Get A Twitter, Facebook And Google+ Account!...24

Create A Facebook Call To Action Tab!...25

Post Daily On Your Social Media Accounts!...26

Learn How To Properly Use Your Social Media Accounts!...27

Open A Pinterest Account And Start Pinning!...28

Start And Continue A Blog! Blog, Baby, Blog!...29

Put On An Education Seminar For Free!...31

Host An Event At Your Office!...32

Have A Grand Opening Event!...33

Get Out And Network Once A Week!...34

Learn How To Network!...35

Start A Weekly Information E-Mail Newsletter!...36

Get A Website! What? You Have A Website?...38

Learn Search Engine Optimization (Seo)!...40

Create A List Of Keywords!...42

Fix Your Website!...43

Add G.A.S. To Your Website!...44

Create A Microsite(S)!...45

Get Involved In Your Community!...47

Adopt A Street!...48

Write And Submit A Social Media Press Release!...49

Join A Toastmasters Group!...50

Open An Audible Account!...51

Listen To Read A Business Book A Week!...52

Get A Table At An Expo!...53

Present A Seminar At An Expo!...54

Sign Up For Haro!...55

Write Articles For Publications!...56

Get And Ezinearticles.Com Account!...57

Submit An Ezine Article!...58

Open A Hootsuite Account!...59

Start A Mastermind Group!...60

Attend A Speed Networking Event!...61

Send A Thank You Letter To The People You Met!...62

Create A Database Of Birthdays And Anniversaries!...63

Send Birthday Cards To Your Clients!...64

Open A Youtube Channel!...65

Post A Youtube Video!...66

Create A New And Improved Logo!...67

Teach A Seminar Or Class At A Local College!...68

Produce A How-To Report!...69

Write A Book!...70

Publish A Book On Lulu!...71

Publish Your Book On Kindle!...72

Carry Your Book Everywhere You Go!...73

Dedicate Your Book To A Potential Client!...74

Record A Cd Program!...75

Add E-Mail Sign-Up Form To Your Website & Blog!...76

Call A Business Acquaintance And Just Say Hi!...77

Carry Business Cards Everywhere You Go!...78

Attend A Seminar On Your Subject!...79

Attend A Seminar That's Not On Your Subject!...80

Open A Basecamp Account!...81

Add A Project To Your Basecamp Account!...82

Take A Wordpress Web Design Class!...83

Build The Microsite!...84

Print Promotional Items For Your Business!...85

Determine How You Will Create Top-Of-Mind Awareness!...86

Revamp Your "Elevator Speech" (3 Seconds)!...88

Write Ten Ways You Provide Value To Clients!...89

Make A Coffee Appointment With A Business Stranger!...90

Change The Signature File On Your Outlook Program!...91

Watch James Wedmore's Youtube Videos!...92

Record A Video Testimonial!...93

Read Seth Godin's "Permission Marketing" Book!...94

Open A Send Out Cards Account!...95

Ask Someone How You Can Help Them With Their Business!...96

Send 10 Hand-Written Thank You Notes!...97

Read Your Haro Email!...98

Respond To A Haro Query!...99

Take A CEO To Lunch!...100

Get A Professional Headshot Taken!...101

Change Your Linkedin Profile Picture!...102

Create A Professional Looking Banner For Fb, Twitter, Linkedin, Google+ ...103

Smile! Take A Break! Drink Water!...104

Wear "Happy Socks!"...106

Attend An Industry Conference!...107

Create A Hot List Of Potential Clients!...108

Don't Sell, Market!...109

Open A Zoho Account! Zoho Is A CRM, Customer Relationship Management....110

Watch A How To Use CRM Video!...111

Understand Content Marketing!...112

Join A Meetup.Com Group!...113

Create A Powerpoint Presentation!...114

Open A Slideshare.Net Account And Post Your Presentation!...115

Share Your Slideshare.Net Presentation On Social Media! Slideshare.Net Is Your Level 1 Tool....116

Close Facebook And Outlook On Your Pc!...117

Watch An Episode Or Two Of Shark Tank And The Profit!...118

Create A Qr Code For Your Business!...118

Raise Your Prices!...120

Have Three Price Levels!...121

Fire Troubled Clients!...122

Understand And Measure ROI!...123

Understand Your Unique Selling Proposition -USP!...124

Barter Your Products And Services!...125

Market With A Friend Or Network Of Friends!...126

Don't "Compete" Cooperate!...127

Hug Your Clients!...128

Do It Right Now! God Bless You! And Happy Marketing! Thank You!

Preface

Marketing has changed! We are in the era of New Media and New Marketing. This is the best time ever to massively grow your business and enjoy great success. But holding on to your old-school marketing ways will keep you stalled or can even destroy your business!

In this book, I show you over 100 innovative New Media and New Marketing ways to market your business, increase your revenue and explode your profit with minimal costs.

To get the best out of this book be willing to learn and prepare to grow your business. Having a desire and motivation plays an essential factor to drive a successful business.

In this book I am going to expand your knowledge with innovative and exhilarating ways to market your business. Prepare yourself for the new and exciting world of new media, new marketing.

I'm going to analyze and provide you a variety of new plans on how to successfully start or massively grow your business. You'll understand how social media companies like Facebook, LinkedIn, Twitter and Pinterest function for your business and you'll learn about other tools that can help you succeed, efficiently reduce time and annihilate in competition.

The Marketing Magic Workshop is designed for professional and entrepreneurs interested in obtaining new information to start and succeed in new or existing business ventures. So get ready to experience over 100 new and innovative ways to grow your business and experience Marketing Magic!

#1

Mystify Your Audience with Great Customer Service

I am always surprised on how bad the customer service is truly out there.

One of the great differentiators is amazing or remarkable customer service. If you provide great customer service, people will talk about you, your reviews online will be fabulous and you will get more business referred to you. Why? Because you will be at the top of your game and apart from everyone else.

There is such a lack of service nowadays that you can certainly differentiate yourself from your competitors by going above and beyond. Here are some examples of great customer service:

Publix Supermarkets: Ask a store employee where a specific item is and they will not just tell you but they will take you to the item(s).

Chick-fil-A: Your order is completed promptly. They call you by name. The restaurant is always clean. The drive through employees gets your order to you quickly and correct. Chick-fil-A is an amazing place. I tell everyone about them in my courses, in this book and one-on-one.

I don't see customer service improving anytime soon! Which means that if you consider this a marketing tool and you create an atmosphere of providing excellent customer service you will create a following and your business will grow through word-of-mouth.

#2

Under Promise and Over Deliver

This goes back to the same concept of customer service, a providing remarkable customer service. Remarkable means "worth making a remark about."

Under promise: Example: when you provide information and your completion date, for example, to your potential or existing client, provide a date and then meet it or beat it.

Over deliver: Example: Add something else of value to your product or service. Add something unexpected to what you offer or what you give in return for your fees.

Under promise and over deliver, it is an amazing marketing tool.

#3

Zig when they Zag

I have heard this from a friend of mine many years ago, Randy Gage. He said, "Zig when they zag." As an example, I use Every Door Direct Mail (EDDM), It is direct mail marketing, using the U.S. Post Office at a reduced cost to very targeted areas. Why? Because no one else is doing it!

Everybody is going online: social media, Facebook and everything else online. Stay informed and stay educated on the latest marketing tools available to grow your business. It's not necessarily Social Media. But on the social media front, try Pinterest. Pinterest converts much better than most other social media tools.

Try guerilla marketing! These are different and unique ways to get your products and services known.

Zig when they zag! Do it differently than they do.

#4

Use Every Door Direct Mail EDDM

Remember when I said "Zig when they Zag?"

Well, every door direct mail for 18 1/2 cents/piece, they can reach every door on the postal carrier's route. Imagine that with a great direct mail piece that does not have to be small, it can actually big: 8 1/2 x 11 or so. Go to every door direct mail, USPS. Make sure you have the USPS website and start using Every Door Direct Mail. You have a minimum of 200 pieces. If I want to send 500 pieces, which I do often, usually about once a month that is about $90 somewhat. What a great deal! I can target a very specific area, delivering to every door every 24-48 hours after I take the pieces to the post office.

Guess what? No addressing, no permits, no additional fees. It is amazing. Business owners are slowly starting to get the idea of this great service offered by the post office.

I offer every door direct mail to my clients as a marketing service, as a marketing idea, as a marketing tool. Every Door Direct Mail works. Try it.

#5

Join a Chamber of Commerce

You may or may not know that I am the President of the Doral Chamber of Commerce in Miami, Florida. What I recommend is find a good chamber of commerce. One that is practical with events and meet new business people.

Network, get involved and as I tell my new chamber members: show up. If you show up at a good and practical chamber of commerce, you will get new businesses. It is like a gym membership, you pay for it. If you don't show up, you don't see results.

Meeting people and keeping a database and contact with those professionals is one of the most important things you should do! Build your database on Constant Contact and LinkedIn.

Don't try to sell to the people you meet at chamber of commerce events! Build relationships! This creates top-of-mind awareness of you and your business. Help others grow their business by referring other professionals to them! This practice will grow your business.

#6

Build Relationships

This takes us to the G.A.S. formula. It is about building relationships in the new world of new media. With all the technology, and social media sites, and online marketing and all this and all that, it is really about building relationships more than ever.

People buy from people they know, people they trust and people they perceived as experts. Build those relationships first before you even sell. Think about marketing instead of selling.

G.A.S. stands for:

Give Knowledge

Answer Questions

Solve Problems

Create content and information to give away via your website, blog, email and videos. Share this content freely, and also on your social media platforms such as LinkedIn, Facebook, Twitter, Pinterest and Google+.

The G.A.S. builds relationships and creates top-of-mind awareness. They will remember you and how and where to find you when they need to refer business to you.

#7

Understand How Social Media Really Works

We talk about social media.

How does social media really work? It is not about having a Facebook account. It is not about having a Twitter account. You know what? People are not listening to those accounts anyways.

Unless you have a cute kitten, an adorable puppy or a video of someone smashing themselves into the wall and bleeding, no one is listening on these tools. So be very careful to put all your eggs in the social media basket.

Understand how social media really works. It is about what I call the G.A.S. formula: give knowledge, answer questions and solve problems. It is about the C.C.E formula: Capture-Call to Action-Engagement. Consider that and understand how social media really works for you. Learn the right way and not just pushing information out there.

Social Media should be divided in two levels. I call them M-Levels™:

Level 1 – Content creation are tools such as:

Website, Blog, YouTube, Social Media Press Releases, Document Sharing, LinkedIn Articles.

Level 2 – Sharing tools such as:

Facebook, Twitter, LinkedIn, Google+, Pinterest, Social Bookmarking

Publish on Level 1 tools and share on as many Level 2 tools as possible. The result is a saturation of your content and Google's perception of you as an authority, bringing your content to the top of the search engine result pages. Remember to use keywords on titles, content, tags and image file names.

#8

Get A LinkedIn Profile

LinkedIn is a much better tool than Facebook and most other social media sites. A lot of people do not have a LinkedIn account. Many professionals do not have a LinkedIn account. Why is that? That is one of the best and most practical tools that you can have. What do you do on LinkedIn? I will tell you more about that in a bit.

#9

Join 10 Groups On Linkedin

You can join up to 50 groups on LinkedIn, but you do not want to be in 50 groups because you are not going to be active on all those groups. I want you to be active. Which leads me to the next Marketing Magic Idea...

#10

Participate In 2 Discussions on LinkedIn Groups

Participate in two discussions at least per week or more. One per day would be fantastic. Yes, it is time consuming, but the return on investment of your time by participating in groups and discussions is powerful because you are actually building those relationships and getting your.

I want you to participate in the discussions, or even, create discussions on LinkedIn groups.

Discussions should be real, not spam! Create or participate in discussions where you can demonstrate your knowledge and expertise. You want to illicit responses and a discussion on your topic, so don't be afraid to be a bit controversial and to speak on hot topics.

Remember, it's about building relationships.

#11

Get A Twitter, Facebook And Google+ Account

I want you to have a Twitter, Facebook and Google+ account done the right way. With proper, keyword-rich profiles and branded with banners, professional profile photos and logos. Remember that a personal account is a personal account on Facebook, and you create "pages" for your business.

Understand how they work and how they function. Use the "Call to Action" button. Get on Twitter. Get on the social media accounts that are actually active, the ones where your target market hangs out. Of course, we must go back to LinkedIn. The best social media tool for building business connections.

Keep an eye on Google+. We don't know where it's heading. But for right now, it still continues to be strong. Add your 5000 people to your circles strategically. They will see your posts if they add you to their circles. Google local listings now include the ability to post. Optimize your local Google business listing and start posting.

#12

Create A Facebook Call To Action Tab

Now you can do that on your Facebook page as you can do it on your personal page. It is amazing that Facebook actually gives us a call to action tab or button because now people can click on that button and go to your website. Click on that button and go to some type of capture mechanism or conversion location, where real connections actually happen. That makes Facebook practical, where it was not in the past.

I heard someone say the other day that Facebook is a business, not a social media tool! That's so true. Facebook's goal is to get you to buy ads, which in my opinion and experience, never work.

#13

Post Daily On Your Social Media Accounts

I get a big, "Oh, man! How do I do that? How am I supposed to do that? It is so time consuming to post daily on social media!"

There are a lot of shortcuts tools I use to post on social media sites. My prime choice is Constant Contact that has a tool called Social Share. Whereas when you create an event or you send out an email, then you could schedule postings via Social Share. With several clicks you can schedule multiple posts on multiple days to multiple sites.

Other shortcut tools include Hootsuite, where you can also schedule multiple posts and also track your timelines, mentions and hashtags. You can download apps for your browsers that allow you to post directly from your browser, such as Pinterest, Hootlet, Delicious and others.

Make it easy for visitors to post from your site or blog by installing share buttons or plugins.

#14

Learn How To Properly Use Your Social Media Accounts

Consider that you have two levels of social media. I call them Level-1 and Level-2 social media accounts, also known as M-Levels™. You post your content on Level-1 social media accounts and share those postings on Level-2 social media accounts.

What are your level 1s by the way? Level-1s are blog postings, YouTube videos, Slide Share presentations, LinkedIn Articles, Social Media Press Releases like PRLog and even content on your website. That's Level-1 social media.

Then you share those Level-1 postings on your Level-2s: Twitter, LinkedIn, Facebook, Pinterest, etc., your social media marketing tools. That is proper way to use social media.

In most cases when you post on Level-2s directly your posts are never seen.

#15

Open A Pinterest Account And Start Pinning

Your target market is on Pinterest. It is an amazing social media marketing tool. Use Pinterest to find great information on absolutely everything, yes, everything. Recipes, car mechanics, graphics, arts and crafts, animals, home improvement, business, and most anything you can think of.

Pinterest is an incredible tool. Guess what? The right target market is on Pinterest: the decision makers.

Who are the decision makers? Women! They are very active on Pinterest, which is a lot different than Facebook and Twitter. Pinterest is a lot of fun and very practical. It is for personal use and for business use. Pinterest can get your target market to your website. It is one of the best sites for getting direct traffic to your website and conversions. Open a Pinterest account and start pinning right away.

#16

Start And Continue A Blog! Blog, Baby, Blog!

You must have a blog if you want traffic to your business. Just make sure that you continue posting once you start your blog. I say continue because there are millions and millions of orphan blogs. People start a blog and never continue it. It is not challenging to post on blogs. It is not that challenging to start a blog.

You can use tools like Blogger, which takes you 5 minutes to start a blog. It is very simple. Now, wordpress.com is a much more powerful blogging tool but the learning curve is a little bit significant. So, start on blogger.com with your Google account. Start blogging.

Learn SEO because the titles must contain keywords. The keywords become the URLs and sometimes they are converted to H1 tags or Headers. Google loves H1 tags.

The content in your blog is very important. Use keywords in your content and keep it to 3-7 paragraphs. Longer blogs tend to get more Google love but they don't get read as much.

By the way, all of your blog postings are considered Level-1 social media content. Your blog postings should contain media such as images or videos. The images and other media should be optimized too. For example, image file names should be changed to keyword-keyword-keyword.png. You can learn more about SEO in my simple SEO course at Udemy.com.

#17

Put On An Education Seminar For Free

Where you can do these seminars? At your local chamber of commerce, Rotary Clubs, or at any opportunity that you given to put on a free event. A lot of the universities will let you come in and do a free event. Of course, you have to have a marketing aspect of it so you can get people in the door. Some press releases can do that for you to the local media. Post on the local media calendars and create an event on Eventbrite and Meetup.com.

Put on an event because education-based marketing or seminar marketing is one of the best, most important tools that you can use. I do this all the time. Your goal is to put on an amazing, information-filled workshop where at the end of the seminar or workshop, they come to you and they say, "Hey, how can I do business with you? How can I do this? Do you do this? Do you do that? Can I have your business card?"

Side note here: never push your business card on people in networking events or in any place else. Make sure that you only give it to them when they ask you for it. Don't be a Card Pusher.

#18

Host An Event At Your Office

The reason I like events because events are high SEO tools online, like Eventbrite and Meetup.com.

Constantly optimized tools like Eventbrite can get traffic to your website. But guess what? On Eventbrite, you have a profile. People can click on your profile and go to your website.

Do an event at your office. Use any excuse: grand opening, one year anniversary, two year anniversary, something I like to call a business blitz, just invite them over for a coffee. The best time to do an event at your office is during the day, 8am to 10am. Tuesdays, Wednesdays and Thursdays are the best days to host them.

When you have an event or a networking event at your office you are inviting people into your world. It breaks the ice. You build relationships, remember that, and you can potentially get new clients.

What happens is that the paradigm of people changes when they meet you at your office. It is a different story. It is a different you. It is a more personal you and you build relationships and top of mind awareness by hosting an event at your office.

#19

Have A Grand Opening Event

You mean you haven't done a Grand Opening event yet? What are you waiting for? Let's have your grand opening. Have a great celebration. Invite the mayor. Most mayors in most cities will come to your opening event as long as you schedule it with time. Grand opening events are typically done Tuesday, Wednesday, or Thursday in the afternoon, late afternoon like 5:30 pm.

Of course, if you have some beverages and food that is even better. It is a great opportunity, especially if you promote it through a chamber and get their support for marketing. List the grand opening on Eventbrite, Meetup and all the other local calendar events. Send a Press Release to your local media. You may get coverage and great exposure for your business.

#20

Get Out And Network Once A Week

Find some events to attend every week. It does not matter what kind of event. What I tell my chamber members and my clients is that does not matter what the event is, just go to an event once a week, network and get to know other professionals.

#21

Learn How To Network

You go to networking events but what do you do? Push cards on people's faces. No! That is not how you do it! Build relationships first! Sounds familiar? Get to know the people you meet at these events. How? By asking questions.

Bryan Tracy says when you know someone and meet somebody in a networking event, what you ask him or her is, "If I have to recommend someone to you, what would I have to know about you?"

Let them answer that question and then ask them another question, then ask them another question. You wait until it comes back to you. Never push your card. You never give away your card until someone asks you for it. And even then I still want you to focus on the other person.

Business comes from building relationships first. In most cases it's not the person you meet where the business comes from. It's from the people they know – from their network of business connections. The only way they will remember or want to refer business to you is to become top-of-mind to them. You are the first one who comes to mind when asked for your particular product or service!

Build relationships first.

#22

Start A Weekly Informational E-Mail Newsletter

Guess how many client e-mails I started with? One. I am now at 45,000 opt-in e-mails, Over 50 social media sites and 9,000 Meetup.com members. It took a long time to build my database but that database now responds when I send an email. My emails are usually informational, or mostly about upcoming events. I get responses, sign ups and I create top-of-mind awareness. They click on the links inside the e-mail. They respond and show up to our events. We fill up events with email marketing.

Start collecting e-mails. Start building databases. The value of your business is determined by the quality, and quantity of your databases.

The best kinds of emails to send are newsletters with real, quality, practical and useful information for your target market. Informational newsletters provide what I termed the G.A.S: Give knowledge, Answers questions and Solve problems. Provide G.A.S. content. Don't sell in your email. Maybe a small coupon on the bottom of the email with a special offer but that is about it.

Send emails to your list on a weekly basis. If you don't send for months, people forget about you. They opt out or even report you as spam when they receive an email from you months down the road. Set the expectation. Do NOT spam.

Use Constant Contact, which is really a great tool. With that, you are going to start building relationships and people will start to get to know you AND REMEMBER YOU.

#23

Get A Website! What? You Have A Website?

You won't believe that about a 50-60% of business owners or companies still do not have a website. When they do, it's a badly built, ugly website with zero SEO optimization and an awful user experience (UX).

Get a nice, keyword-rich, target market, relevant website that has a call to action, a caption mechanism and some type of engagement tools. If you do that, that website no longer has to cause you tons of money. Use WordPress to build your website(s). It's a simple tool that is SEO friendly, aesthetically pleasing and you can have a professional looking website that you control, at very little cost.

Learn how to build websites and have a professional-looking, productive, lead-capturing website that looks for good for your business and is functional. It does not have to be fancy anymore and get rid of the swish, the zoom and have plenty of white space on your site.

Make sure your website gets people the call to action. Make your website visitors move through your website by giving them a call to action. Don't load up your pages with so much content that users give up on the page. You need to get people to move through your website in order to get Google Love!

Optimizing a WordPress created website is simple with included SEO plugins and tools.

Create niche websites. It's ok to have several websites. Use them to differentiate your different product lines and services. Niche, or as I like to call them, micro-websites can get indexed faster by Google so that they appear at the top of searches.

#24

Learn Search Engine Optimization (SEO)

SEO means optimizing your website for Google's algorithms, a fancy word for the mathematical calculations that Google makes on their servers to determine which page to serve up in response to a Google search query.

But SEO is also affected by everything you do with your social media, your blogging and your content creation. "Content is king" is an old cliché that is very true in SEO. You must create content that is keyword-rich and SEO optimized. Google loves this content!

Learn real SEO techniques. Be careful with third party "SEO experts." If somebody promises you #1 on Google "for only" whatever amount, just say "no thank you". Because they can't fulfill such promises! Even I, who has been studying SEO for years, can't promise you #1 on Google.

But if you learn good SEO techniques, you will be able to optimize your website, optimize your social media including your Facebook and your LinkedIn content, blogs, videos and even images. Then you'll have a presence online that Google can't ignore. You will have what Google calls "authority."

When your target market types the correct keyword, they will find your website, your blog, your video, your slideshow presentation. Learn SEO.

#25

Create A List Of Keywords

Build a master list of keywords for SEO. You are going to live and die by this list of keywords. Rather, your business will live or die by the use f this list. Proper keywords from the master list on all those social media tools previously mentioned and you have a fantastic opportunity to be at the top of the searches like Bing, Yahoo! And Google.

I cover keyword research on my "Simple SEO" course on Udemy. You can learn more about my courses at the end of the book.

#26

Fix Your Website

Now that you understand SEO, fix your website. Fix your Title tag, your Description tag even the Keyword tags, and your image file names and alt-tags. Optimize at least your old tags or if you can upload new images. Optimize the keywords in the images before you upload them.

Write proper H1 and H2 tags with proper keywords. Optimize your permalinks if it is a new site or if you are adding pages. Permalinks are your URLs. There's a whole checklist in my course "Simple-SEO" on Udemy.com.

Download the free checklist and you can follow all the details of your website and makes your website better optimized. By the way, keep something in mind: April of last year, Google came up with a new algorithm so if your website is not mobile ready. It will downgrade your site in mobile phone. If you are building your website make sure that's it's responsive. Make sure it is mobile ready. Typically, responsive is mobile ready and you can verify that on Google.

#27

Add G.A.S. To Your Website

Here we go, back to building relationships. Give knowledge, Answer questions, and Solve problems. Why is your target market looking for on Google?

They are looking for knowledge. So, give them knowledge on your website proactively. They are looking for Answers to their questions. So, Answer their questions proactively on your website. They are looking for solutions to their problems. So, Solve their problems proactively on your website, on your blog, on your YouTube video. That is what your target market is searching for.

They are looking for G.A.S. Give them the G.A.S. The result is that you build relationships. Second result is, probably the first result is you get to the top of searches when someone searches the right keywords. Third, they remember you or bookmark you. And fourth, they refer business to you! Helping you grow your business.

#28

Create A Microsite(s)

I mentioned previously that you could do everything that I teach in my SEO class, follow everything Google teaches you about SEO, and for some reason you cannot get on top of the search engine result pages.

This I call, mysteries of the Google Universe! Here is one solution: create a micro-site or several micro-sites. I do this all the time! I teach WordPress! We originally marketed WordPress throughout the chamber of commerce website and throughout a newmedianewmarketing.com's website. We were not really getting the results we wanted. When we did the keyword research, we found that most people search for WordPress training and WordPress classes. So we searched for an available .com domain that contained those keywords, preferably in that order.

While the exact domains were not available, WordPressTrainingAndClasses.com was. I grabbed that domain and created a simple SEO optimized website with the top searched keywords we found by doing a keyword research.

Now we have the WordPress training in Miami, WordPress training in Lakeland, WordPress training in Doral, even WordPress training in Orlando. So, we purchased several domains for those areas and created niched micro-sites.

The result is that we are on the top of the search results because of these microsites. A microsite is just specifically for that niche market. The narrower you can get the niche, the greater the chance of appearing at the top of search results on the search engines.

It is one of the fantastic tips that I can give you that can really get you to the top of the searches.

#29

Get Involved In Your Community

There are many local programs where the city and the community need your help. Autism Speaks, March of Dimes, community park events, wherein a lot of times you can get involved for free or promote your business by getting involved for minimal cost.

Most of the park departments need help especially in smaller cities. The parks department is your target market. Get involved. Give back. I think we have the responsibility to give back anyways. So, get involved. What is going to happen is that you are going to build these relationships with amazing people, with the amazing parents whose children participate in park programs. Those amazing parents are business owners. Get involved in the community and give back.

#30

Adopt A Street

This is a winner. Imagine renting a billboard for the entire year at no cost to you. You can adopt a street in most cities at no cost to you. Just complete an application. Send it in to the responsible person at public works. They submit it to the council. The council and the mayor vote on it. If you get approved, you get a beautiful street sign on each end of one-mile strip of road. I have adopted a very important street here in my city of Doral. I am going to have a sign that says, "Sponsored by or Street Adopted by New Media, New Marketing."

Wow, that's very valuable free marketing! That street alone gets thousands of cars travelling through every day. It is like a free billboard. Adopt a street. Just call your local city and get your hands on some valuable, free marketing.

#31

Write And Submit A Social Media Press Release

What is a Social Media Press Release? You've probably never heard of it because every time I go to a social media class, webinar, seminar or read a book, no one talks about it. PRLog.org is the main site that I suggest for submitting Social Media Press Releases.

PRLog is a social media press release. It does not go out to the media but it is a keyword rich, SEO optimized tool that shows up on search results all the time. It is a Level-1 tool. It's an amazing way to provide content that is picked up by the search engines.

Write a keyword-rich, target market press release that talks about your business, something notable or one of your social media efforts. Submit it on PRLog.org and 24-7PressRelease.com. Then you share across all your social media Level-2 sites: LinkedIn, Facebook, Twitter, your social bookmarking sites, etc. It is an amazing tool for free traffic to your website and links to your website, especially PRLog.org.

#32

Join A Toastmasters Group

Number one fear in the world is public speaking. At your local Toastmasters group you practice public speaking. For a small annual fee, you can join a group in your neighborhood. Toastmasters groups are comprised of professional. Your target markets is in these groups. It's a tribe. It's a very tight knit group. If you become a part of that tribe, you will be able to build new business. It just opens doors for you with people you never thought would be in these Toastmasters group: people from Fortune 500 companies, local companies, etc.

Join the Toastmasters group. It is great! By the way, they are available all hours of the day in all cities, everywhere you go, morning, noon, night, English, Spanish, etc. Join a Toastmasters group today.

#33

Open An Audible Account

Why Audible? It is an audio books website now owned by Amazon. When you graduate, you get an MBA. But don't stop there. You get your bachelor's. Don't stop there. Life is changing. Technology is changing. Marketing is changing. Sales are changing. Businesses are changing. You've got to keep up with the latest technologies.

At Audible.com you can download the latest audio book, business audio book, and listen to it while you drive, while you are in a car, while you are in a public transportation, while you sleep or while you go to sleep. I should say. I even listen in the shower. I listen to at least about one audio book a week. That makes 52 business books a year. Imagine what you can do if you have a knowledge of 52 business books a year. Get an Audible account. You can get the first one or two audiobooks for free and start learning.

You can learn the equivalent of an MBA education if you focus on constant learning. Education changes the game. Since marketing and technology changes daily you will be way ahead of your competition.

#34

Listen To Read A Business Book A Week

Like I said, I listen to a business book a week, at least. Download that audio book or buy a book, read that book. Kindle is an amazing tool. Many business books are free on Kindle. Especially if you join Prime on Amazon! Download and read or listen to a book a week. It is going to change your life, specifically, your business life.

#35

Get A Table At An Expo

Get a table at a business expo. They are sometimes called tabletop expos. By displaying your brochures and business cards, and giving away promotional items, you have access to 500 to 1500 people that are attentive and open for conversation. It's a great way to market your business. You can also walk around to the other vendors and create more business relationships. It is typically very inexpensive: $150 to $500 to rent a table or booth at a local tabletop expo or local business expo. Expos are an excellent marketing tool.

#36

Present A Seminar At An Expo

Many of these expos let you present a seminar or workshop. Some are free. Present your seminar. Present your workshop. Hopefully, the promoters will do a great job in promoting these seminars or workshops and you will get 10 to 100 people in attendance. Present a seminar. Remember education-based marketing is one of the best marketing tools in the new world of new marketing.

#37

Sign Up For Haro

You've probably have never heard of HARO. HARO is www.helpareporterout.com. When you sign up for HARO you will receive an email or two each day with reporters looking to interview professionals like you. It's a free service. Sign up for HARO. Select your preferences. Read the daily emails. Read the queries of interest to you. Submit a query to whoever is looking to interview a person with your experience.

There are all kinds of topics from technology to medical, etc. So, sign up for HARO. It's one of the best tools to get free publicity on major publications and media.

#38

Write Articles For Publications

If you can, look for opportunity to write for publications. Publications like the Huffington Post are often looking for local writers in your area of expertise. Look for local newspapers. They are looking for people to write on specific topics. There are many publications. You are not going to get paid in most cases. But that is okay.

This is a good PR. Just make sure to put a byline and information about you on the bottom of that article and enjoy the results of being considered the expert in your field.

#39

Get An Ezinearticles.Com Account

Want to find others to post articles on their website or blog for you? Go to Ezinearticles.com and open an account. In Ezinearticles.com you can publish articles for free and other website owners, blog owners can pick up your content, post it on their website or blog. They cannot edit it. They have to post it as is.

The bottom of those ezinearticles.com articles contains your tag line. Of course, they can click through your profile, potentially getting you new business. Your job in these articles is to demonstrate expertise and that is what you are doing with Ezinearticles.

Ezinearticles.com is also a great Google SEO tool because when someone posts your article on their website with the link back to your website (called a backlink) Google counts towards SEO, towards valuing and ranking your website higher in the search results.

Ezinearticles.com has over 30,000,000 million monthly visitors. The website is searchable so it is a fantastic source of traffic to your website and a great source of business connections.

#40

Submit An Ezine Article

You've got to get active on ezinearticles.com. Just having an Ezinearticle.com account doesn't do you any good unless you publish! If you like to write, that's even better. You don't have to write. There are many ways to do it. Recording and then transcribing, etc. So, submit an E-zine article at least one or two a month. You will see the results.

Ezinearticles are Level-1 social media tools, which you them post on all your Level-2 social media sites. Watch the traffic to your website begin to grow.

#41

Open A Hootsuite Account

As I mentioned earlier, I want to post on social media every day. Well, Hootsuite makes it easy for you to post every day because you can schedule. You can post one time and schedule several times to several of your social media accounts. Keep in mind though that if you are using Constant Contact, it's easier to schedule then on Hootsuite.

Constant Contact's tool is called Social Share. It's part of your Constant Contact account. Post an event at Constant Contact and then scroll down the page to Social Share. Social Share has a better scheduling system than Hootsuite. You can schedule all days at once versus Hootsuite where you have to actually schedule one then click back and schedule again.

Hootsuite can also be used to monitor your social media timelines, hashtags, mentions and specific words on your social media accounts.

#42

Start A Mastermind Group

If you are going to start a Mastermind group, follow the rules and the steps in *Think and Grow Rich*. This is a system that really works. It's amazing what happens when you get together like-minded individuals and you consult with each other and give responsibilities with each other plus provide accountability for each other.

Getting a Mastermind group or even creating one is a fantastic tool. You meet once a week, share ideas. Just make sure that you follow the guidelines in *Think and Grow Rich*. You don't have to buy the book because it is online.

Start a Mastermind group; your life is going to change.

#43

Attend A Speed Networking Event

Speed Networking is one of our signature events at our chamber, the Doral Chamber of Commerce. This is fantastic tool where you get to meet people with no B.S, no dilly-dallying around talking about what you are going to do tonight. It is two minutes where you talk about your business and the other person talks about their business; period! The bell rings and one side moves over to the next person.

It's like speed dating. But it's Speed Networking. You can gather 25-50 business contacts in a one to 2 hour Speed Networking session. It's a fantastic tool for meeting other professionals. So, attend a local speed-networking event and bring plenty of business cards with you!

#44

Send A Thank You Letter To The People You Met

Send a thank you letter to the people you met in a networking event or speed networking event. It is a differentiator and a game changer. You want to Zig when they Zag. No one is doing it. So, you do it.

Thank you letters or thank you notes are fantastic tools. I will talk to you about send out cards and some other tools where you can do it semi-automated, but hand-written thank you notes have a greater impact.

#45

Create A Database Of Birthdays And Anniversaries

Build a database with the birthdays and anniversaries of your clients and then send them a birthday, anniversary or special event card. Again, it's unexpected. It's a game changer. It's a business builder.

Nowadays it's become too easy to say Happy Birthday on Facebook. Although it's ok to do that, a handwritten birthday card has a tremendous impact on building relationships and creating top-of-mind awareness of you to potential clients or referring professionals.

#46

Send Birthday Cards To Your Clients

See #45. That goes to what we just said. You got to gather the birthdates first, of course. Then send them the birthday cards, and send them anniversary cards. You will see an amazing result.

People are going to be amazed that you actually did that for them. You are going to differentiate yourself. You are going to separate yourself because you are zigging when they are zagging. I know this is repetitious. But it's a very important tip worth repeating. Just Do It!

#47

Open A YouTube Channel

YouTube is the number two search engine in the world, number three most traffic website in the world, and growing in active viewers and uploads. YouTube is its own search engine. It makes a huge difference to your business when you create a YouTube channel and when you post on YouTube.

YouTube channel can be a branded across the top and you can have an introductory promotional video on the main page. Learn how this is done. It's very simple. So, open a YouTube channel right away.

#48

Post A YouTube Video

You got to post on your YouTube channel. Just having a channel alone is not going to do anything for you. But knowing that it is the number two search engine in the world, number three most trafficked website in the world should give you a clue that posting YouTube videos in extremely important to your marketing efforts! When you upload a video that is properly optimized, the keywords in the title, the keywords in the content, and those tags and labels, make your video findable on a YouTube and sometimes Google search

More and more searches are being conducted on YouTube. You must find a way to create a video marketing strategy and post on YouTube, Facebook and other video sites.

#49

Create A New And Improved Logo

Let's change your brand. Why don't you create and improve your logo? Is your logo out of date? Is your logo old school looking? It is time to change. Liven-up! Even Walmart changed their logo. Why did they change their brand? Life changes, business changes, and you want to re-brand yourself at times. So create a new and improved logo. It doesn't cost that much to create a logo.

#50

Teach A Seminar Or Class At A Local College

If you want to teach in an MBA class, you have to have an MBA. Community schools, colleges and high schools will let you teach a class on whatever it is that you're an expert on, your expertise: writing, social media, business, finance, anything that you know that you can teach at a local university or college. Do it! This is a great way to build relationships and you will get some businesses from it.

I take every opportunity to teach courses, seminars and workshops. I have several groups of employment-challenged individuals where I go and run a free LinkedIn class for them. Often times, when they get back on their feet they come back to us and take the rest of our courses. But the important part is to give back! Remember, it goes back to giving back to the community but also when you are teaching at a university or college, you are building that rapport, you are building those relationships and you are giving back.

#51

Produce A How-To Report

I told you about having to capture contacts and building databases. We call it the CCE: Capture, Call to Action and Engagement. Well, people are not going to give you their email for nothing, right? So create a how-to report that is really useful information of 10, 15, 20 pages that you can give as an ethical bribe. So people give you their email in exchange for your report. This how-to report should be evergreen, which means that it's timeless and you can use it today, next month, even next year without having to update it. You can print it and give it out in a seminar or workshop.

You can give it out as a branding tool or you give it out in exchange for someone giving you his or her email. So you can capture their emails and put it on the email-marketing database and get them on a marketing newsletter.

Another thing that you can do with that e-mail marketing, if you can capture on your website, you can set it on auto-responder where they get a series of emails automatically sent to them when that email is captured. Constant Contact is a great tool to do that with.

#52

Write A Book

It is easier than ever to write a book. If you do not like to write, that is okay because you can transcribe it. If you do not like to transcribe, that's okay. You can have somebody interview you. Most of us have this knowledge inside us.

It's as easy as getting in front of the microphone, recording it and sending it for transcription. I had two books transcribed of 100 pages or more in Kenya. I found the person through Elance for $48 and hired them to transcribe my 2 1/2 hour workshops. I had it recorded in mp3, on a mini recorder. Once the transcription is complete all you have to do is editing. Publishing a book is just a series of simple steps. It is easier than ever because you can self-publish. You no longer need a publishing house.

The result of having a book as that now you can call yourself a "published author" and show up with copies of your book to sell or giveaway at your workshops or seminars. Imagine that instead of a business card you give a potential client a copy of your book. Would it make a difference in getting the client? Of course it would!

#53

Publish A Book On Lulu or CreateSpace

Lulu.com and CreateSpace are free to publish. Did you hear that? They are free to publish. It does not cost you anything to publish. Forget about getting a major company to pick up your book or give you an advance. It's not going to happen. You have to prove that you can sell your book first before a major publishing company will pick you up.

A literary agent will not touch you because of your reputation, and theirs. So, you've got to be published first and demonstrate your sales. Side tip here: when you publish on Lulu.com or CreateSpace, make sure you have an ISBN number because with the ISBN number these literary agents and these publishing houses can track how many books you've actually sold.

They can tell how many Amazon sales and Barnes and Noble sales went through with the ISBN number. You can self-publish and print a book and have either order one book or order a thousand books. You no longer have to buy a thousand books and keep them in your garage or closet hoping to sell them.

Publishing your own book is a game changer!

#54

Publish Your Book On Kindle

That same book can be published on Lulu.com or CreateSpace can be instantly published on Kindle.

It takes a little bit of formatting but it's simple to do. There are many people on Upwork (formerly "Elance") that can do this for you at a very inexpensive price because it's a very simple editing.

Kindle Direct Publishing is a free service from Amazon, as is CreateSpace. You can publish for free and you can make as much as 70% royalties on Kindle Books you publish. You publish the physical book on Lulu.com or CreateSpace (Print on Demand – POD) and publish your book on Kindle Direct Publishing. It's instant income!

#55

Carry Your Book Everywhere You Go

You must have two things with you everywhere you go from now on; a book under your arm and a sharpie on your pocket. Don't pull out a business card when you meet someone at a networking event. Put it inside your book. Offer them a copy of your "new" book and offer to "dedicate it". You can them who to dedicate the book to. It impresses them more to receive a free copy of your book then to get a business card from you they never even asked for.

Now they are potentially doing business with a published author versus a card pusher. You give away your book and you build a relationship and top-of-mind awareness of you… the published author.

Next, take out another book and put it under your arm. Don't forget the sharpie.

#56

Dedicate Your Book To A Potential Client

What will happen is amazing. Everybody else around that potential client is going to be watching you. Wow there's a published author. Let me go talk to this person! He or she must be important. Guess what happens next?

#57

Record A CD Program

That book can be turned into a CD Program, a DVD Programs or an online course. The great thing about the CD and DVD programs or even online courses like Udemy.com is that it's a new system of distribution of your expertise or knowledge that people will pay money for.

Online courses are exploding in popularity. You need to be involved in creating online courses based on your expertise. Everything you know and topics that you have knowledge of or can research can be a course. They can make you money and help you grow your business.

#58

Add E-Mail Sign-Up Form To Your Website & Blog

I mentioned this tip before under the C.C.E. formula; Capture, Call to Action, Engagement. Add an email sign-up form to your website and blog. Make sure your capture is effective by only asking for Name and Email and providing an ethical bribe in return for completing the signup form.

they complete the form they get set up in an auto-responder series. Give them a great series of great G.A.S. lessons for a week or two weeks, every other day or every other week. This will create top-of-mind awareness of you, your product or service.

#59

Call A Business Acquaintance And Just Say Hi

For no real reason, call a business acquaintance and just say hi! It is going to blow their mind if you call. I want you to get into a habit every week of making these calls. Call someone and say, "Hi, John! Hey, how are you? How's business? How is your wife? How is this? How is that?"

Just call and say hi. Build relationships, especially your clients. You need to keep in touch. Maybe you have not spoken to a client for months. Call them up and just say hi. Sometimes we don't call existing clients because we fear that they are not happy with our product or service. If that is the case, then you need to re-examine your products and services and create a dynamic, remarkable product or service that provides tremendous value.

#60

Carry Business Cards Everywhere You Go

Don't be a business card pusher. Don't shove business cards in people's faces. Never take out your business card until they ask you for one. Strange to hear that, I know because we've been taught that business cards should be given to anyone and everyone you meet. That's just not the case.

I'm sure that you've experienced that annoying person that comes up to you in a networking event and pushes a card into your face. "Hi, I am this. I am that." You know, my first feeling is, "Hey, I don't care." That's what most people are typically thinking. They just don't care. You tend to shut them off if you lead with a business card and "what you do" first. So don't pull out your business card until they've asked you, but have them with you everywhere you go at all times.

Remember to build relationships first by asking questions and genuinely caring to know and understand the other person first.

#61

Attend A Seminar On Your Subject

Learn, learn, learn, and learn some more!

This is important. Life is changing. Business is changing. Marketing is changing. Sales are changing. This is what it's called New Media, in marketing, New Marketing. This is the new era of business life that we're in right now. Everything has changed. So, keep up on your topic.

You are an "expert" in your field. With the speed of change in knowledge and technology accelerating at a lighting pace, if you don't continue to educate your self you will be left behind. You'll also need this knowledge to create content as your Level-1 content for your websites, blogs and other social media tools, and share on your Level-2 social media sites.

These seminars are also a great way to build your network of business professionals.

#62

Attend A Seminar That's Not On Your Subject

I challenge you to do this. Attend a seminar that has nothing to do with what you do. Why should I go there? Because it will open your mind to new opportunities, new ventures and new relationships. You've got to move your mindset away from the stagnant to new views of the world. This opens up creative channels in your mind that will trickle down to your current business. You will create new ideas, new points of view and new growth opportunities.

Get to know new people in a different industry. Learn and build relationships. This is about meeting new people and creating new ideas and new growth.

#63

Open A Basecamp Account

Basecamp is a project management tool, a very simple management tool that will change your life. It changed mine. Why? Because it has made me better organized.

With Basecamp you can assign projects and to dos. You can create and manage multiple projects efficiently. You can also follow up on what's getting done and what's not getting done.

It is an amazing tool. For the most part, it is free. Open a Basecamp.com account today.

#64

Add A Project To Your Basecamp Account

I want you to add a project immediately and invite people to Basecamp and specific projects they will be working on. Why? If you don't get into the habit of using Basecamp right away you will not use it at all.

Basecamp has been a business enhancing and growth tool. I manage all my projects on Basecamp.com because it enables me to be a more efficient CEO.

#65

Take A WordPress Web Design Class

It is easy to build amazing, beautiful, professional concept, mobile friendly websites with WordPress. I teach a WordPress class live in Miami and also have my course on Udemy.com Students learn to build amazing sites. Now, every time I need a website now, I don't have pay someone to do it.

I just go on WordPress, get my domain on 1and1.com Internet hosting, install WordPress, push a couple of buttons, add content and voila, my website is built.

Obviously, or sometimes not that obvious, every business needs a professional and functional website for their business. Unfortunately, it's extremely challenging and costly to find a good website designer. WordPress fixes this issue.

Everybody in our offices knows how to build websites or make change to our existing websites. So, learn WordPress. It is an amazing, simple, professional tool to build functional and aesthetically pleasing websites.

#66

Build The Microsite

Build the microsite that we talked about earlier. With WordPress it's easy to create a website everytime you need one. If you have any other target markets, build a microsite. You can link them together and create a link-wheel. Link-wheels create inbound and outbound links to all your websites. Google loves these links and that helps you with SEO and rankings on Google, Bing and Yahoo search engines.

So, build a microsite. It is easy to do with WordPress. Your microsite should have a minimum of five to six pages that are SEO optimized with the proper keywords. Follow the SEO Checklist from my SEO course at Udemy.com for other optimization tips.

#67

Print Promotional Items For Your Business

Be very selective. Print only promotional items that people are going to keep even if it cost you more. That means think about what the person is going to ultimately do with the promotional item. Are they going to keep it? Are they going to use it? Are they going to toss it?

How many pens do we get when we go to a networking event or a business expo? Those little cheap plastic pens are thrown away? How does that help you? Don't do it!

Print and distribute promotional items that people will remember you by. One promotional item that is costly but very good giveaways are USB drives. I have one that is attached to my keychain. It goes with me everywhere I go. It is very memorable and very useful. Order only promotional items that are memorable and that create top-of-mind awareness.

#68

Determine How You Will Create Top-Of-Mind Awareness

This goes back to #67. Here are the details. Determine how you will create a top-of-mind awareness. This is one of the most important things in business right now! Because we are so distracted with tons of information how do you get people to remember you when they are looking for a product or service like yours? You may meet somebody in a networking event and they may or may not need your business now. But, as I've said before, it's not always the person you meet directly that can use your products and services. But they have hundreds of connections; businesses acquaintances and friends that may ask them to refer their contacts to them. So, you've got to build a strategy to be top-of-mind for your target market, especially potential referrals.

Best way to create top-of-mind awareness is to build a rapport using the G.A.S. formula to help others proactively with online and offline content: Give knowledge, Answer questions and Solve problems.

Because you are proactive in asking questions and making your encounter about them, not you, they will remember the encounter. If you go beyond the first contact by communicating the G.A.S. in email newsletters, videos, blogs and other forms, you will become top-of-mind to them.

You've got to make your business remarkable – worth making a remark about! How do they remember you? Well, there are lots of tools to do that. One way that I've already mentioned is exceptional customer service. When they come in the first time to your business, you must be exceptional! You have to be exceptional at all time. This means your employees must be involved in your "remarkable" philosophy of doing business.

Why are so many businesses failing right now? Because they don't commit to excellent customer service! What happens when I encounter excellent customer service? I talk about a business and sometimes use them as examples? When do most people talk about a business? When they experience an issue with a company.

Any one for Cracker Barrel? Why? Cracker Barrel is remarkable, remarkable food, remarkable value, and remarkable service. Why can't other restaurants do it the Cracker Barrell way? I ask myself that all the time. Answer: Because they just don't care to.

Let's talk fast food. The words fast food and remarkable don't usually go together. Except in the case of Chick-fil-A. Chick-fil-A is remarkable.

At Chick-fil-A your order is completed promptly. They call you by your name. The restaurant is always clean. The drive through employees get your order to you quickly and correct. Chick-fil-A is an amazing place. I tell everyone about them in my courses, in this book and one-on-one.

So, determine how you will create a top-of-mind by making your business remarkable! Because on of the best top-of-mind tools is excellent customer service.

#69

Revamp Your "Elevator Speech" (3 Seconds)

No, you don't have 30 seconds for your "elevator pitch." You have 3 seconds!

Make those 3 seconds about them. Sounds strange? Well it shouldn't. I've been saying this throughout this entire book. So, lets change your "elevator pitch". A realtor typically says; "My name is John and I'm a realtor." Boom! Your mind shuts off. Instead, try, "I help you find the home of your dreams." Isn't that simple? Isn't that powerful? Yes, it is. It touches their emotions and gets their attention. Your whole idea of your pitch should be to elicit a response from them; "Really? How do you do that?"

People do not want to be sold anything. People want to be understood and they don't mind buying from you. People buy from people they like, know, trust and perceive as experts, but you have build a relationship first, or else nothing happens.

You run across someone in networking event and your elevator speech goes on, "Yes, cause we are great. We have been in the business for 20 years. We have sold this many homes..." No one cares about how many home you've sold or how many employees you have! They're thinking about how to get rid of you. So, revamp your three-second-elevator speech and make it about them. Try; "I help you...." It works!

#70

Write Ten Ways You Provide Value To Clients

If you think about it, your products and services are designed to provide value and to help people. I want you to write ten ways that you provide value with your products and services. How do you make their lives better? How do you make their lives easier? How do you help them be more efficient? How do you help them have a better family life? How do you provide value to your clients?

The reason I want you to make a list is because I want you to have to think about how you provide value. Because that's your number 1 responsibility: providing value. Write that list! That is going to be such an important exercise for you. It is going to change the way you think about marketing your products and services.

#71

Make A Coffee Appointment With A Business Stranger

At every networking event I tell the professionals in attendance about making two coffee appointments with two people you they haven't met yet. I tell them to make the coffee appointment sooner than later. The same day if possible. I tell them that when they meet for coffee, make sure the place serves very hot coffee, like Starbucks. "Don't buy the little shots of espressos because you'll finish it too fast." I want them to spend time getting to know that person and asking them questions. Asking them how they do it, why they do it, how they got into the business.

One great question to ask that breaks the ice and builds relationships is "If I have to recommend someone to you, how would I describe your product or business to them?" How do I explain you, your products and services?

Make two coffee appointments today and start building two new relationships.

#72

Change The Signature File On Your Outlook Program

A lot of people leave that out. Did you know that you can add images on the bottom of your email signature and that it could be linked to your website URL? Add links to your LinkedIn account, Facebook, and YouTube channel. Make it interesting. Put your logo or your professional headshot on the signature box. It is a free marketing that you are most likely missing out on.

#73

Watch James Wedmore's YouTube Videos

James Wedmore teaches you YouTube video marketing. He provides a lot of great information for free on his YouTube channel and website. He's got programs you can buy that provide even more extensive knowledge on video marketing for your business. He is going to change how you think about video marketing. He is going to get rid of your fears and make it easy for you to start growing your business through video marketing.

#74

Record A Video Testimonial

All you do is to have your iPhone with you and ask an attendee at your workshop or seminar if they are willing to give you a testimonial.

Turn the video record mode on your iPhone on and start recording. If you want to get more intricate, you can buy a tripod adaptor and a wired lavaliere microphone for your iPhone.

Do not worry about background noise. It's okay. We are getting a testimonial, and people expect that because you're at an event. Just make sure that you can hear the interviewed person clearly.

There are only two secrets about video recording; lights and sound. Make sure the lighting in bright and make sure the sound is clear! Videos don't have to be perfect. It's no longer expected. In fact, crude videos seem to be better received by today's audience, as long as the speaker is sincere and the topic is interesting. Keep testimonial video to 2:00 minutes or less.

#75

Read Seth Godin's "Permission Marketing" Book

It is an old book but it's dead on. Typically, I tell you that do not buy an old book because it is out of date. Well, this book was actually way ahead of its time. Seth talks about things like being remarkable, worth making a remark about and other useful topics for your business.

Remember Disney's philosophy: Do things so well so uniquely and people cannot help telling others about you. That was a Disney philosophy. Run with it! It changes your business. It changes your life. So does Seth Godin's "Permission Marketing" book. Seth Godin has many other books that will change your life and the way you think about business.

#76

Open A Send Out Cards Account

We are almost there! Remember that I told you to send anniversary card, birthday card and thank you notes? Well, send out cards is a way to do it. It is easy, inexpensive and it helps you get rid of the excuse of sending out these cards because you can schedule the birthday, anniversary or other special occasion cards. So, open a send out cards account and start building relationships today!

Here is a link to SendOut Cards: www.sendoutcards.com

#77

Ask Someone How You Can Help Them With Their Business

You know, you have to change your concept of what business is all about… and what life is all about! We have a responsibility in this earth. Our responsibility is to help others. This is not some spiritual mumbojumbo. Sometimes people need help and you can provide it. It is not all about the dollars. We need to make money and I am not pro-poverty by any extremes. The more we make money, the more we can help others.

If you are in a good place and even if you are not, ask someone else how you can help him or her with the business. Volunteer for an hour and help them do something. Help them record a video, help them write a book, help them do something. Get outside of yourself and things will change for you. Besides that, you build relationships.

#78

Send 10 Hand-Written Thank You Notes

I asked you previously to sign up for SendOutCards.com. This is good for scheduling birthdays and anniversary or special occasions greeting cards. But hand-written greeting cards are a game changer.

Go to your local stationary store and buy some nice thank you notes and hand write 10 of them to your existing clients. Feel free to insert your business card. People are going to be amazed at receiving them. You are going to differentiate yourself from others and you will be remembered. You are going to strengthen relationships and build top-of-mind awareness. Send hand-written thank you notes to clients or potential clients, people who have done great things for you! It's a game-changer.

#79

Read Your Haro Email

Do not forget to go back and read your HARO email because you've probably received great queries. You may be able to submit and be interviewed for USA Today or some other major publication. Go back and read your HARO account.

#80

Respond To A Haro Query

Reading your HARO emails is not enough! Go back to your HARO emails and find just one query to respond to. I know that this sounds repetitious, but I want you to take action on HARO because if one publication publishes an article on you it can have a dramatic impact on your business. It's very simple; they just give you an email and guidelines to respond to the query.

You should give them a paragraph or two, nothing complex; you are not going to write a long query letter. You're just going to write a simple response to the letter. If they want you and interview you, you could have some great, free publicity.

#81

Take A CEO To Lunch

Do not be afraid. The first time I did that I called my friend, Randy. I was having struggles with the business.

I said, "Randy, can I take you to lunch?"

He said, "Oh, no. I do not eat lunch."

"Well, you eat breakfast, don't you?"

"Yeah, I eat across the street."

"Okay, I will meet you there. What time and what date?"

We went to breakfast and he gave me two hours of amazing information. We could not make the breakfast but he did meet me for lunch. It cost me a $120 to feed this guy but I tell you what, it was thousands and thousands of dollars of fantastic information from his genius-marketing brain. I left the lunch and my life change.

So, take a CEO to lunch and you will be surprised of the outcome of the encounter.

#82

Get A Professional Headshot Taken

Have you seen a shot of shadow man or shadow woman on LinkedIn? That's a big no-no! Have you seen a company logo on your personal profile? That's another no-no!

Get a professional head shot taken. Surprisingly, it's not that expensive. Sometimes, you can even do it yourself but I don't suggest you to do that. Find a professional photographer to take the pictures. It will cost you $100 to $250 for the session. You will end up a great 10, 15 headshots for your LinkedIn, website and other social media profiles.

You want to be viewed, as a professional so don't use your Glamour Shots or high school graduation picture! It's a sure way to lose out on business! Get a professional headshot taken as soon as possible.

#83

Change Your Linkedin Profile Picture

If you have the picture from your high school graduation with the cap and gown, it's definitely the wrong picture. Change it to that new, professional looking headshot you just had made. LinkedIn is a professional tool that potential clients use to find out the truth about you. What does your profile picture say about you? So, change your LinkedIn profile picture immediately.

#84

Create A Professional Looking Banner For Fb, Twitter, Linkedin, Google+

I'll give you a tip of where you can have this done for $5. It's called Fiverr.com. It's amazing the work that they can do for you for $5. Sometimes they'll charge you a bit more, depending on the options available.

Depending on the gig provider on Fiverr.com, they give you original images or various images. Get one that provides the Photoshop files (.PSD) so you have control of more changes if you decide to make them without paying more money.

They know all the sizes; you do not have to figure out the sizes. Upload them on your accounts. You'll have a more professional looking profile in all these sites, especially LinkedIn.

#85

Smile! Take A Break! Drink Water

Relax and get out of town! You have to break away from the 24/7. I am a 24/7 person but sometimes, I get on the road to Orlando because Mickey is my favorite buddy. I visit him all the time. Why? Because the Turnpike is my stress releaser. I'm working my tail off. I am working hard on building my business, creating courses for you, working hard writing books! But I take breaks. Maybe not as often as I'd like, or as often as I should. But I do take them.

Find what your stress relief is. What's your stress breaker? The thing that will get you away from it all and bring you back to peace and a relax mind.

When I am on the highway heading on to North Orlando, I am having a fun time. All of a sudden, about halfway there, I take a deep breath and I'm totally relaxed. My laptop is in the trunk of my car but I'm still relaxing! Just take a break. Be careful with your health and your sanity.

With our stressful ways we tend to get dehydrated. We don't drink enough water and we not feed ourselves properly. Make sure you are taking care of your nutrition. Water is the life element. Make sure you drink plenty of water. Stay away from unhealthy food. Being sick and rich is not the best way to be.

P.S. Smile on purpose! It releases endorphins and provides for better health.

#86

Wear "Happy Socks"

Wear "Happy Socks" today! So, there's actually a brand called "Happy Socks." I bought that brand because on the socks themselves it says "Happy Socks". They have all kinds of colors and stripes, yellows, polka dots, black and white, reds, flowers, hearts (my favorite), etc…

I put them on in the morning and during the day I remember I have them on. I smile and I get happy. So wear Happy Socks. I know this sounds weird but who cares? You need to get away from stress and the stuff that you go through every day. So, wear "Happy Socks." Who cares what "they" think! You know how you feel – Happy!

#87

Attend An Industry Conference

Attend a workshop for your industry. It's important that you get out and learn and be educated on the latest products, services and concepts in your industry. It's called constant learning and never ending improvement. You might have heard of it. It's a great concept that changes your life! You should always be learning and keeping up with your trade, so attend an industry conference.

#88

Create A Hot List Of Potential Clients

Sit down one afternoon and create your Dream List. Which clients would you like to have? Somehow, as if by magic, you begin to make the phone calls you need to and you start making the right connections.

You begin to do the right things to attract your Dream List to your business. So, create this Dream List of potential clients and post it up on near your computer so you can view it daily.

I like to print my list formatted elegantly with Word and put it on the wall. So, create a Dream List of potential clients and you will soon attract them to you.

#89

Don't Sell, Market!

This goes back when you present yourself at a networking event. Remember that? Instead of saying, "Hey, I am a card pusher. I am this and I am that," to "I help you do..."

Learn how to market with the "New Marketing". As a matter of fact, get rid of the "S" word. I call it the 4-letter "S" word (Sale or Sell). When you are ready to say the "S" word, change it to the "M" word, Marketing.

Your life will change. Your paradigm of how you market your business will change. So do not sell. Instead, market your products and services. Remember that marketing is about providing value and building relationships.

#90

Open A Zoho Account! Zoho Is A CRM, Customer Relationship Management

Zoho is a CRM tool. CRM stands for Customer Relationship Management. There are many CRMs out there: SalesForce, Zoho, Hubspot, etc. Hubspot CRM is free, easy, and simple to implement and learn. You just need tools to implement is and start using it.

Hubspot CRM helps you keep track of your leads. It is so important because the biggest fail in marketing our business, on building new clients, is the follow-up. We fail on follow-up, which is often the most important thing we should be doing to build our business.

Hubspot is a CRM system that helps you by giving you a simple, yet powerful, follow-up system. Open a Hubspot CRM account today.

#91

Watch A How To Use CRM Video

There are plenty of videos out there on using CRMs and specific CRM systems. Hubspot is free and a very powerful tool to grow your business, but if you don't use the system it won't do you much good. It is going to change your business.

You must insist that your staff use the CRM. It will mean thousands of dollars' worth of business if you implement and use Hubspot or another CRM. It can mean failure if you don't.

#92

Understand Content Marketing

In this new world of new media and new marketing, it's all about content creation! You have to create keyword rich, target market, relevant content and place that on the appropriate tools such as blogs, website, YouTube, Slideshare, LinkedIn, etc. Remember those are your Level-1 social media profiles that I spoke about earlier. Then you are going to share that Level-1 content on your Level-2s.

Your content has to have media within. It means keyword rich optimized image or video. The success of your business is going to be online. Content marketing in the tool that will help you build relationships, communicate with potential clients and create new business.

It goes back to the G.A.S: Give knowledge, Answer questions, and Solve problems. Understand content marketing and start creating valuable keyword-rich, relevant content that helps your target market.

#93

Join A Meetup.Com Group

Meetup has been around since 2002. I have been on Meetup.com hosting 3 groups since 2006. If you are interested in Chihuahuas, you can join a Meetup group for Chihuahua lovers. I'm not kidding. There are Meetup.com groups for any interest.

Join Meetup.com and find groups of your interest, or better yet, your target market. Attend meet-ups and get to know new people. It is easier to do business with people who are just like you and have the same interest than people who are not and do not have the same interest as you do.

Seriously, if you like Chihuahuas join Meetup. Search Chihuahuas in your area and you are going to find Chihuahua meet up groups. I am not kidding. Check it out for yourself. Better yet, search for groups where potentially your target market hangs out. Join the group and attend the Meetups.

Meetup.com is a great tool and it's free to join. There is a fee to create and host groups.

#94

Create A PowerPoint Presentation

You probably have PowerPoint presentations that you've used to present your business. If you do not, start creating them. It is easy to do. There are plenty of tutorials online. Microsoft.com has beautiful templates that you can use to create professional PowerPoint presentations. Just click on New and find templates on Microsoft.com. These PowerPoint presentations are Level-1 "content." Upload the presentations to slideshare.net and allow them to be displayed on your LinkedIn account.

#95

Open A Slideshare.Net Account And Post Your Presentation

The content of the PowerPoint presentation should be optimized for the keyword. So create a PowerPoint presentation and upload it to slideshare.net, then share that across your Level-2 social media sites such as Facebook, Twitter, Pinterest, Google+ and others.

This is a really good tip to build professional relationships. Don't skip this one.

Make sure that your PowerPoint has a keyword-optimized title, keyword optimized content and labels (keywords). This is very important! Slideshare.net is a social media tool. It builds community. People will start following you. Every time you post a new PowerPoint presentation on SlideShare.net they get notification that you have a new PowerPoint presentation. So, you build a very strong community of professionals.

Slideshare.net presentations appear on search results all the time, making it a powerful SEO tool for business.

#96

Share Your Slideshare.Net Presentation On Social Media!

Slideshare.net presentations are Level-1 social media content. You are going to share your slideshare.net presentations across your Level-2 social media tools. Some of these tools are; Twitter, LinkedIn, Facebook, social bookmarking sites, etc. It is going to make a major difference because Google is going to start seeing your slideshare.net presentation and content all over the Internet.

It also builds links back to your website. Google is going to start giving you Google Love as we call it and ranking you higher, and sometimes ranking your slideshow presentation higher than your website.

#97

Close Facebook And Outlook On Your PC

In the morning, don't open your email or Facebook accounts first thing. I heard this said in one of the business book by Brian Tracy, "your email is somebody else's agenda for you." So if the first thing you do in the morning is open up Facebook and Outlook, then it is going to reacting to those e-mails and Facebook posts, making you very inefficient.

You should be setting your agenda yourself. Then sometimes later on in the morning, that is when you are going to open your Outlook and start responding.

Be careful. Facebook is an addictive site. You go in there for two minutes and you end up lost in the Facebook abyss for hours.

Don't open up Facebook and Outlook until later in the morning.

#98

Watch An Episode Or Two Of Shark Tank And The Profit

If you've not seen these shows, especially Shark Tank, you must. You can catch them online. You can catch them on YouTube or on-demand.

You are going to learn so much watching these shows. Shark Tank will change the way you think about business. It is also going to amaze you. It's incredible to see what kind of products and services actually sell. You'll also get ideas to start a business.

You will learn business tools, business tips and how to present your business to potential investors and even potential clients. Watch an episode or two of Shark Tank and The Profit.

#99

Create A QR Code For Your Business

QR codes are branding tools or conversation piece. QR stands for Quick Response Code. They've been around since 1994 but now it is when they have come to fruition. So have it on your business card and have it in your materials.

People are going to scan and go directly to your website or even directly to your YouTube video. It is an amazing tool so learn about QR codes and implement them into your marketing strategy.

QR codes are also a conversation starter. People will ask you what the QR code on your business card is. Use it as a conversation starter or icebreaker as you demonstrate how the QR code works.

#100

Raise Your Prices

Raise your prices? Are you crazy? An amazing thing happened to me. Sometimes we fear raising prices, believing that if we raise prices we will lose clients. The truth is that the opposite can actually happen? It has happened to me.

We were teaching QuickBooks locally charging a fee of $127. It was just too cheap because another business offered the course for $295 and $395. We finally ended up raising it to $147 and our attendance increased.

We are still the lowest price in the market and we are sometimes misconstrued as an inferior product. But we are making greater profits. The other benefit of raising our prices is that the quality of our clients increased. We don't get the tire kickers any more.

Raise your prices. Don't be afraid! You might just be pleasantly surprised at the outcome.

BONUS #101

Have Three Price Levels

This psychologically works. You have three price levels. The middle price level is the price at which you'd like people to buy your products and services. You offer a cheaper price and a more expensive price. Psychologically, people do not want to pay the cheaper price because they think, "Hey this must be a cheaper product." They do not want to end up with a higher price. The result is that most of the time they'll buy the middle price choice.

By the way you should exaggerate the higher price a bit and you will be surprise that sometimes you'll sell it. So, have three price levels for your products and services.

BONUS #102

Fire Troubled Clients

Do the math. Sometimes you are doing so much work that you are actually working for $10/hour. This tip is often so difficult and so challenging to business owners because they're afraid to lose business.

Do not be afraid to fire troubled clients. Be nice. Always be nice. What you can do is to refer them to someone else. "Hey Mr. Jones, you know, we kind of change the way we do business now. I think it is time for us to move on. I think you might be better with Joe Mo down the street who could actually provide you with the service you deserve."

Move them all along. Don't be afraid. Even when shopping for new clients, don't be afraid to say no. If you see trouble from the beginning, you are going to get trouble at the end, so don't be afraid to say no to clients.

Firing these troubled clients will open up more time and resources so that you can provide higher quality service to your other clients. The result is more business and greater peace of mind for you.

BONUS #103

Understand And Measure ROI

I am going to give you a simple formula. If you make $1 more in profits than what you spend on a specific campaign such as AdWords, Facebook ads, even every door direct mail, that is a positive return on investment (ROI).

If you have positive ROI on a specific investment you run more ads. If you get negative ROI you stop running ads. Don't run online ads for more that a week without testing. You can run it for two or three days and find out if you are getting a positive return on investment or not.

A client came to me and told me that they were going to run a $3,000 budget for the month on Adwords. I said, "Woah, stop!" You do not have to. Try it for 3, 4, 5 days and spend a $100 and see what the response is.

Can you get conversion? Can you get positive ROI? That's the key. The great thing we have right now in marketing is instant feedback. We do not have to spend tons of money to find out if something works because we can tell instantly. It is really great. It's amazing.

Stop spending money needlessly on any type of marketing. Measure ROI then decide to either change the media or invest more on the one you're tested.

BONUS #104

Understand Your Unique Selling Proposition - USP

What differentiates you? Many people are doing the same thing you do. Your marketing message has to tell people what you do differently and how you do it differently and why they should do business with you versus your competition. You've got to put some thought into your USP. Forget about calling it USP, it's too technical.

What differentiates you from other potential vendors? That has to be in your marketing message. That has to be portrayed in all your marketing tools. What makes you different? Why you over your competitor? Make sure you understand your USP and understand how to explain to potential clients why you are better than your competition.

BONUS #105

Barter Your Products And Services

You will be surprised what you get from bartering. You can get products and services where you spend tons of money on. Anything and everything can be bartered: printing, Internet services, web design, etc. What you provide is very valuable to someone else. Bartering cost you a lot less so look into trading your products and services. Just make sure that the deal is in writing.

BONUS #106

Market With A Friend Or Network Of Friends

This helps when you go to a networking event because it is going to help you feel more comfortable. It is going to motivate you to go to more events. Your friends will hold you accountable for going or not going. So, network with friends.

At a networking event, don't hang out with your friend. Separate yourself.

Another reason to network with friends is that they can help you get rid with the cling-ons. I am not talking about Star Trek. I am talking about people will come to you and "cling on." They are trying to push their wares, and push the business cards. Watch each other from across the room and if a cling-on appears go over to your friend and say, "Hey John, come with me. I need you to meet someone."

So market with a friend or network of friends makes networking events easier and more effective.

BONUS #107

Don't "Compete", Cooperate

If you worry so much about competition, you are going to spend so much energy on trying to defeat your competition rather than improving your products and services.

Often times you can actually work with your competition and have more peace of mind. Your mind is more open to creating businesses when you work together rather than trying to compete.

I work with other chambers of commerce and I make sure I help them promote their seminars and workshops. With reciprocity, they come back and help me promote my workshops and services.

Don't think competition, think cooperation.

BONUS #108

Hug Your Clients

Hug everyone. I do it. Now, it is going to be easier in our culture in Miami because we are kind of used to doing this. Be careful with other cultures. You can get smacked into the face if you try to hug the wrong person.

I show real, sincere appreciation, sincere care for someone else, for business people especially for our clients and chamber members. So, you are going to see me hugging everybody.

If it's only a fist pump is all you can muster, then so be it.

Don't be the one with the cold fish handshake! Be different. Hug someone and you are going to see major things happen because you become a real person rather than another stiff.

BONUS #109

Do It Right Now! God Bless You! And Happy Marketing!

Thank You!

About the Author

Emmanuel "Manny" Sarmiento is the CEO and Co-Founder of the Doral Chamber of Commerce. He is also CEO of New Media, New Marketing, Inc., an Internet and Social Media Marketing consulting, outsourcing and education company, since 2009, and The StartUp Annex™, a unique business incubator based in Miami, Florida.

With over 500 Social Media, Internet Marketing courses, marketing workshops and seminars, including the Social media University and the Certified Social Media Marketing Specialist(TM) program, Manny has become the Master of Social Media Marketing training, education and implementation and business startups.

Manny has created and implemented Entrepreneurship and Business Education programs that help develop the skills of business owners and executives. He teaches Business and Marketing skills to entrepreneurs to help create prosperity in their business and in their lives. He has been teaching Web Optimization, Search Engine Optimization (SEO), Social Media, Marketing, WordPress and other marketing and business skills since 2007, and has operated businesses in Doral, Florida, since 2005, with great success and dedication to helping others.

Manny attended Miami Dade College and Florida International University and is attending the University of Life, getting his Masters in business mastery and everyday life!

For more information and courses by Manny Sarmiento visit at:

www.udemy.com/simple-seo

www.udemy.com/marketing-magic

Use Promo Code MarketingMagic for a discount!

www.ingramcontent.com/pod-product-compliance
Lightning Source LLC
Chambersburg PA
CBHW060613200326
41521CB00007B/765